Rejoicing in Truth

Written and Illustrated by
Ron and Rebekah Coriell

Fleming H. Revell Company
Old Tappan, New Jersey

© 1980 Fleming H. Revell Company
All rights reserved.
Printed in the United States of America

Honesty
tree

Truthful Words and Ways

Wherefore putting away lying, speak every man truth with his neighbour....
                  Ephesians 4:25

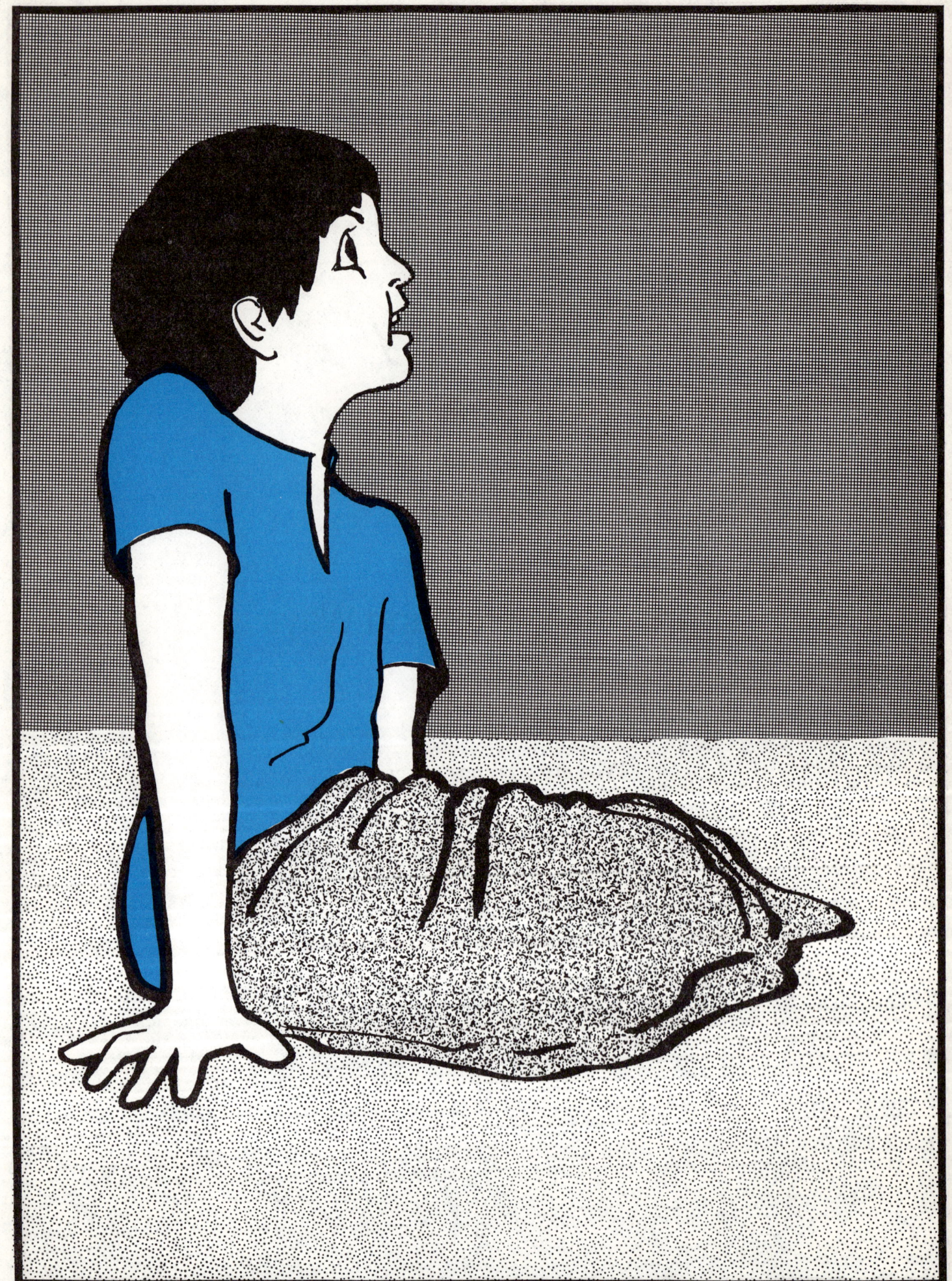

Honesty in the Bible

The people of Israel needed an honest man to lead them, one who would be truthful in his words and ways. The high priest Eli was supposed to fill this need, but he did not. He was old and weak and had not raised his sons Hophni and Phinehas to be honest priests. They stole meat from those who made sacrifices to God. They would demand more than their share of the oxen or sheep that were killed. So poor was the example set by Hophni and Phinehas and Eli that many people began to worship idols. Israel was suffering under dishonest leadership.

At this same time there lived in the land a devout Hebrew named Elkanah. It was his yearly custom to travel to the tabernacle at Shiloh. There he would worship and make sacrifice to God. His wife's name was Hannah and she, too, loved God. But Hannah was barren. "So Hannah rose up after they had eaten in Shiloh, and after they had drunk. Now Eli the priest sat upon a seat by a post of the temple of the Lord. And she was in bitterness of soul, and prayed unto the Lord, and wept bitterly" (1 Samuel 1:9, 10).

To be without child was especially grievous to Hebrew women. Only by bearing a male heir could the family name be continued. Plus, each mother secretly hoped that she might be the one to bear the promised Messiah.

"And she vowed a vow, and said, O Lord of hosts, if thou wilt . . . give unto thine handmaid a male child, then I will give him unto the Lord all the days of his life, and there shall no razor come upon his head" (1 Samuel 1:11).

Eli observed her as she prayed silently, only moving her lips. Mistakenly, he thought she was drunk and he reproved her.

She replied, "Count not thine handmaid as a wicked woman; for out of the abundance of my complaint and grief have I been speaking" (1 Samuel 1:16).

Eli responded, "Go in peace: and the God of Israel grant thee thy petition that thou hast asked of him" (1 Samuel 1:17).

Hannah returned to her husband much encouraged and soon God blessed her with the answer to her prayer. A son was born to them and they called him Samuel, which means, "asked of God."

When the child was old enough to be separated from his mother, he was taken to the tabernacle. His parents had promised to give Samuel back to

God and they were people who kept their word. Thus, they presented their beloved son to the high priest Eli. There he would be taught the laws of God and schooled in the service of the tabernacle. They hoped God would someday use Samuel mightily.

The sons of Eli continued to sin against God. They forced people to give them the best portions of the sacrificed meat. They sinned in many ways. Eli was aware of this, but he failed to discipline his sons.

Meanwhile Samuel grew in the love and knowledge of God. He was the doorkeeper of the tabernacle. He memorized portions of the law written by Moses. He cleaned tools, kept candles lit, helped clean the tabernacle, and ran messages for the high priest.

Because of the wickedness in Israel in those days, messages from the Lord were rare. But one night, while everyone was asleep, a voice called out, "Samuel, Samuel!"

Awakened, the young boy replied, "Yes, what is it?" When no one answered immediately, he assumed it must be Eli calling. He arose quickly and ran to him.

"Here I am. What do you want?" asked Samuel.

Still groggy from sleep, Eli replied, "I didn't call you. Go back to bed."

Samuel returned to his cot. "Maybe it was a dream," he thought.

He had just fallen asleep when the voice called again, "Samuel!" Again, the young servant jumped out of bed and ran to Eli.

"Yes?" he asked. "What do you need?"

Half asleep, Eli answered, "My son, I did not call you. Lie down again."

Puzzled, Samuel was sure someone had called his name, but he did not question the high priest's words. He quickly obeyed and returned to his bed.

A third time God called Samuel's name. Again, Samuel ran to Eli and awakened him.

Then Eli realized that God Himself must be speaking to the boy. So he said, "Go and lie down again. If the voice calls out, say 'Yes, Lord, I'm listening.'"

The boy returned to bed wide awake. Samuel had never received a message directly from God and he was too excited to fall asleep.

Once again, God called, "Samuel, Samuel!"

"Yes, Lord, I'm listening," replied the boy instantly. Then God spoke and shared some shocking news: God said He had continually warned Eli about his wickedness and that of his sons. Now he was going to punish them. None of Eli's family would live to be old; they would all die young. While others would prosper, Eli's descendants would be poor and suffer sadness and grief. Their children would be killed violently. God added that both Hophni and Phinehas would die on the same day to be a sign to Eli that all these predictions would surely come true.

Samuel could hardly sleep the rest of the night. Surely Eli would ask him what God's message was.

When morning came, Eli called for his young assistant. The easy thing to do was to not tell the whole truth. But God's Word teaches honesty. Samuel had decided to always be truthful, no matter what the circumstances.

"And Samuel told him everything, and hid nothing from him . . ." (1 Samuel 3:18).

God rewarded Samuel for his honesty and he became a great prophet of God. Because he was truthful in his words and ways, the people of Israel trusted him and allowed him to be their spiritual leader.

This story is found in 1 Samuel 1:1-3:18.

Honesty of a Hero of the Faith

A hush swept over the crowd of dignitaries who had assembled in the great hall. The Emperor leaned forward to be sure he could hear. Leaders from all over Europe fixed their eyes on the solitary figure who stood before them. Fearlessly he began to speak. His voice echoed off the high ceiling as he magnificently defended the words he had been writing in pamphlets and preaching from pulpits. At last, he summarized all he had spoken. "I cannot do otherwise. Here I stand. May God help me, amen."

Martin Luther returned to his seat to await the decision of the judges. In total honesty, he had given reason for his beliefs and actions that so offended the Catholic Church. Now the leaders of the Diet of Worms would discuss what to do with this renegade priest. This conflict between Martin Luther and the Catholic church involved the sale of indulgences. People who had sinned were encouraged to pay money to the priest who would then pronounce that person's sins forgiven. A paper was then given to the sinner recording the transaction. This was called an indulgence. Different sins had different prices. And people were even encouraged to buy forgiveness for their dead relatives or friends whom they believed to be suffering in purgatory.

Martin Luther did not, at first, question the church's right to sell indulgences. But he was aghast at how this practice was abused. Johann Tetzel, an eloquent Dominican friar and high-pressure salesman, came to Wittenburg to sell indulgences.

"If you but drop a penny into the box for such a soul," cried Tetzel, "as soon as you hear the money clink in the chest, the soul flies up to heaven!"

"I will make a hole in his dream!" cried Martin Luther.

Up to his small room he stormed and began at once to prepare a paper, or set of theses, against the granting of indulgences.

At this point, Martin Luther was concerned about truthful words and ways. He could have been content to remain comfortable as a popular and highly respected priest and university professor. But he had to be honest with himself and God. So he spoke out against the dishonesty of Tetzel. He wrote ninety-five statements, or theses.

About midday, October 31, 1517, Martin Luther walked to the Castle

Church with his paper. The very next day would be All Saints Day. Thousands of people would come to the Castle Church built by Frederick the Elector. There, they hoped to see the church relics on display, which Frederick had collected. Martin Luther bravely posted his document on the church door. This was not unusual because the church door was often used as a bulletin board to announce important events; however, Martin Luther's document was very unusual. It spoke out against a popular and profitable practice of the church.

Although his theses were in Latin, they were quickly translated into German. Copies were spread all across Europe.

For a number of years that followed, the church and Martin Luther spoke out against each other. Debate was furious. Martin Luther was eventually excommunicated from the church. In 1521, he was summoned to the Diet at Worms, Germany, to defend his beliefs before the emperor, Charles V.

In front of that powerful court of princes and church leaders stood the poor, powerless, yet honest Martin Luther. He took his stand that day. For his honesty he was banished from his mother church. But, in the years that followed, many agreed to his stand and he became the father of a new denomination.

Character Development Challenges

What Happens to a Liar?

God says He will punish the false tongue or the liar (Psalms 120:3, 4; 119:118). "It is a fearful thing to fall into the hands of the living God" (Hebrews 10:31). Listed below in the left column is a list of liars. Listed in the right column is a list of the consequences they suffered.

Liars	The Consequence
1. Abraham lies about Sarah being his wife. Genesis 12:13.	1. His son and grandson lie. Genesis 26:7; 27:19
2. Rebekah encourages Jacob to lie, insisting she receive the curse of it. Genesis 27:8-14	2. Jacob must flee, after lying. It is not recorded whether Rebekah ever sees her favorite son again. Genesis 27:43
3. Rachel lies to her father about stealing family idols. Genesis 31:35	3. Soon after, she dies giving birth to Benjamin. Genesis 35:16-18
4. Gibeonites could have received mercy like Rahab, but they chose to lie to Joshua. Joshua 9:1-15	4. They become cursed as slaves, hewers of wood, and drawers of water. Joshua 9:20-24
5. Ananias and Sapphira lie about the money. Acts 5:1, 2	5. Find the consequence. Acts 5:5, 10
6. Jacob lies to his father. Genesis 27:8-33	6. Find the consequence. Genesis 27:42-43; 29:21-28
7. Joseph's brothers lie to Jacob. Genesis 37:31-35	7. Find the consequence. Genesis 42:21
8. Peter denies Christ. Luke 22:54-60	8. Find the consequence. Luke 22:61, 62; John 21:15-17

Can you find other examples?

Joy
ahoy

Being Happy Inside and Out

And my soul shall be joyful in the Lord: it shall rejoice in his salvation.
                        Psalms 35:9

Joyfulness in the Bible

Their backs, torn by the whip of the flogger, burned with pain. The sturdy stocks that held their feet apart did not allow them even the privilege of movement. Sitting in the dark and damp dungeon, Paul and Silas now had time to reflect.

Their preaching tour had begun with much hope. Paul's companions on his second great preaching tour were Silas and young Timothy. They were such a great help to his ministry. In Troas a fourth man joined the Gospel team — Luke, a Greek doctor. Having a physician as part of the group was of great benefit to Paul. It is believed that he suffered constantly from some physical affliction.

While at Troas, Paul had a vision. A man stood before him calling for him to come into Macedonia (Europe) and preach the Gospel. Paul recognized this as the direct leading of God and immediately made preparations for the team to sail. He felt confident that where God leads, He also blesses.

Their expectations were high as they entered a chief city of that part of Europe, called Philippi. It was a military city that was populated mostly by Romans. The custom of Paul was to find the Jewish synagogue or church in town. They would wait till the Sabbath day and then attend the services. During the worship period, people in the congregation were allowed to stand up and speak as God led them. This was the opportunity in which Paul sought to preach the Gospel of Jesus Christ.

To their disappointment they could not find a synagogue in Philippi. In fact, they did not see a single Jewish man. Then surprisingly, they found a group of Jewish women near a river north of the city. This was a favorable spot for religious Jews to meet because it provided water for the washing of their hands before prayer.

The leader among the women was Lydia, a wealthy woman who sold cloth to the well-to-do Romans. As Paul shared the Gospel with her, God opened her heart and she received Christ as her Saviour. All of her household who were with her were also saved and baptized. Then she opened her home for Paul and his companions. New excitement captured Paul and his team as they saw God move hearts and give them a home as headquarters.

The apostles joyfully began their work of seeking converts. But as they preached, they were annoyed by a young girl. She was possessed with an evil spirit that allowed her to tell fortunes. She gained much money for her masters as she entertained people with her unusual skills. At last, Paul turned to her and spoke to the spirit. "I command thee in the name of Jesus Christ to come out of her" (Acts 16:18).

In time, her masters became aware that their slave no longer possessed her magical powers. Enraged because their source of income was gone, they quickly inquired about the cause of their loss. It took them little time to find Paul and his friends. They caught and dragged them before the chiefs of police. Luke and Timothy were not taken because they were subordinate to Paul and Silas. Since Roman law did not cover the theft of magical powers, these greedy men made up a charge. They accused Paul and Silas of bringing disorder to the city by their teachings. Shouts of support and accusations rang out from the surrounding crowd. Wanting to appease the accusers and retain law and order, the magistrates or chiefs of police commanded that the offenders be immediately punished. Without trial or hearing, Paul and Silas were stripped and flogged with rods. Then they were picked up and carried to the inner prison to where the worst criminals were kept. Their legs were spread painfully apart and clamped in heavy wooden stocks. A guard was placed outside the dungeon door to stand watch so that no rescue effort would be made.

As Paul and Silas thought about all that had taken place, they wondered at the strange ways of God. They were certain of their calling to preach in Philippi. But their ministry had yielded only a few women converts. Now they were hopelessly jailed, beaten and bleeding. Most people would be discouraged at these circumstances, but not Paul. Inside, untouched by any rod, was a heart of joy. He was suffering for his Saviour. There is no higher calling. Suddenly, the quietness of the jail was pierced by song and praise to God. Prisoners all around woke up in wonder at the joyous sounds.

The ceiling and walls began to shake. Then the earth beneath began a low, long groan. Prisoners ran to the nearest wall to cower in fear. Doors flung open. Shackles fell off their hands and feet. Awakening, the guard froze in fear at the sight of open cells. He knew he was responsible for any escape.

Grabbing a lighted candle, he ran to Paul's cell. There he discovered his prisoners sitting with smiles of assurance etched across their faces. Now he knew that the witness he had heard from these men must be true. He wanted to know that God, too.

"Sirs," he cried, falling at their feet, "what must I do to be saved?" (Acts 16:30).

And they said, "Believe on the Lord Jesus Christ, and thou shalt be saved, and thy house" (Acts 16:31).

Thus Paul spoke the Word of the Lord unto the jailer and his family. Everyone gladly received Christ as their Saviour. Paul then baptized his new converts. Later, they all assembled in the jailer's house within the prison compound. They ate and rejoiced together in their new friendship and their new relationship to Jesus Christ.

The joyfulness of Paul and Silas was the tool God used to win the jailer and his family. Now they, too, could experience true joy through knowing Jesus Christ.

This story is found in Acts 16:9-34.

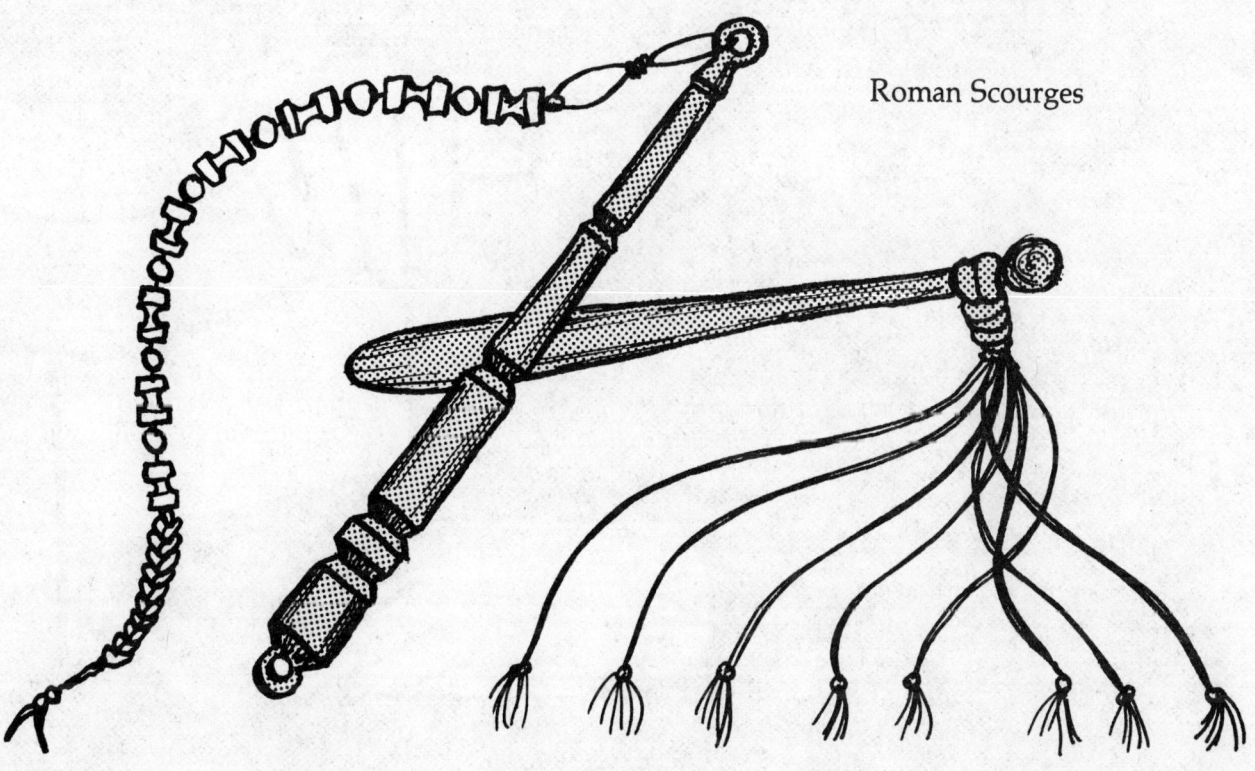

Roman Scourges

Joyfulness
of a Hero of the Faith

It would seem that Fanny Crosby had every reason to be sad and bitter all her life. Six weeks after she was born in 1820, her eyes became inflamed. Her regular doctor was not available so a substitute doctor was called to examine the new Crosby baby's eyes. His diagnosis called for hot poultices but it was a mistake. The result was total blindness for Fanny. She would never again see her mother's face, a flower, or even the sunlight.

In spite of her physical handicap, Fanny Crosby's life evidenced joyfulness, a happiness inside and out. God gave her special grace to overcome her handicap and to excel.

Her early years were spent doing housework, knitting, sewing, playing games and sports, climbing trees, and even riding horses. She accepted her mother's explanation that sometimes the Lord allows one of His special children to go without the sense of sight in order for the child to develop his other senses more fully. In that way a child can help carry out God's special plan for his life.

Fanny's grandmother took her for long walks in the flower-blanketed meadows near her home in southeast New York. Here, she met nature through her senses of touch, hearing, smell, and taste. Her grandmother also spent countless hours reading Scriptures and poetry to an attentive Fanny. So great was her love for this that she memorized much of what she heard. Before she was ten years old, she had memorized the first four books of the Old and New Testaments. She also composed childlike verses of poetry, one of which was published in a county newspaper. It shows what a joyful child she was.

> Oh, what a happy soul I am,
> Although I cannot see,
> I am resolved that in this world
> Contented I will be.
>
> How many blessings I enjoy
> That other people don't!
> So weep or sigh because I'm blind,
> I cannot, and I won't!

When Fanny was fourteen, news was brought to her that caused her heart to burst with excitement. Arrangements had been made for her to attend the New York Institute for the Blind.

She quickly became an excellent student in all her subjects at the Institute, except for math. Regarding that subject, she penned a short verse:

> I loathe, abhor, it makes me sick
> To hear the word arithmetic!

As her schooling progressed, her skill at poetry grew remarkable. On behalf of the school, she was asked on many occasions to recite her poems for prominent people. These included presidents Tyler, Adams, Polk, and Cleveland, and famous senators such as Henry Clay. At the age of twenty-three, she became the first woman to ever address Congress and was given an ovation. Many of her poems were published in newspapers and magazines. In 1844 her first entire book of poetry was published.

It wasn't until Fanny was forty-four years old that she began a career that would make her the most prolific hymn writer of all time. It is estimated that she penned at least eight thousand hymns. Over forty musicians put music to her verses. On two occasions, she "wrote" forty hymns in her head before dictating them to a secretary.

Fanny was widely sought after as a civic, religious, and patriotic speaker. She traveled all over the country to the delight of thousands who thronged to see the blind hymn writer. Her joyful spirit remained always.

Yet, it was in her hymns that her joy was given its most poetic expression.

To God Be the Glory

> Great things He hath taught us, great things He hath done,
> And great our rejoicing thru Jesus the Son;
> But purer and higher and greater will be
> Our wonder, our transport, when Jesus we see.

At one of her last speaking engagements she said about herself, "My dear, dear friends . . . . These ninety years are rich with the wealth of goodness, sparkling with the best spirit of sweetness and overflowing with the true wine of joy and gladness."

Character Development Challenges

Twenty Ways to Increase Joy

Joyfulness is a command from God (Psalms 5:11; Philippians 4:4). In the list below, check the ways *you* are seeking to increase your joy.

1. Confess known sin. Psalms 51:7, 8, 12; 16:11
2. Be obedient to God. John 15:10, 11
3. Read God's Word. Jeremiah 15:16
4. Become a soul winner. Psalms 126:6
5. Control anger; develop meekness. Isaiah 29:19
6. Meditate before sleep. Psalms 63:5, 6
7. Trust God. Psalms 5:11
8. Fear God. Psalms 16:7-9
9. Do right and hate wickedness. Psalms 45:7; 118:15
10. Be humble. Psalms 34:2
11. Seek the Lord. Psalms 40:16
12. Sing unto God. Psalms 71:23
13. Be thankful. Psalms 95:2
14. Pray a psalm back to God. Psalms 95:2
15. Serve the Lord. Psalms 100:2
16. Meditate on Christ. Psalms 104:34
17. Study heroes of the faith. Psalms 107:41-43
18. Write down God's mercy. Psalms 90:14, 15
19. Recognize trials as joy. James 1:2
20. Commit your day to God. Psalms 118:24

Thankful

tankful

**Being Grateful
and Saying So**

In every thing give thanks: for
this is the will of God in
Christ Jesus concerning you.
            1 Thessalonians 5:18

Thankfulness in the Bible

A remarkable thing about God is that He uses the weak to fight the strong. When He does this, He receives all the glory and praise. Deborah was a thankful person who wrote and sang songs to God. She was called to deliver the Jews from oppression.

Because of the sinfulness of the Jews, God decided to chastise them. He allowed the Canaanite King, Jabin, to sweep in from the north with his armies. They quickly occupied the land of the tribes of Naphtali, Zebulun, and Issachar. Using this territory as a base, Jabin intimidated the other nine tribes of Israel and controlled them as he pleased under his general, Sisera. For twenty years Israel suffered the harsh rule of these foreigners.

In desperation, the Jews turned to God and repented of their sins. They cried out in anguish for relief from their persecutors, and God heard them.

Not all the people had forsaken God through the years. Deborah knew God on an intimate basis. God had given her the gift of prophecy. She also was a gifted songwriter. As she sat under the shade of a palm tree, people would seek her help in correcting the problems they had in everyday life. As oppression grew great under Jabin, they asked her to pray to God for deliverance.

Perhaps it was because she was a woman that Jabin allowed her to minister so openly for God among the people. Her songs spoke of God's greatness and His past victories. So contagious was her spirit that all over the land of Israel people began to yearn to be free. Secret preparations were made for an uprising. New chiefs were appointed over the people, replacing, for a time, the local elders. They looked to Deborah for leadership because everyone knew God spoke through her.

Led by God, Deborah sent word to a warrior named Barak. He was to gather an army of ten thousand men and march to Mount Tabor. But Barak's response was disappointing. "If thou wilt go with me, then I will go; but if thou wilt not go with me, then I will not go" (Judges 4:8).

Not to be deterred by the weakness of her general, the prophetess agreed to go. But she let Barak know that he would not get the glory for the victory to come.

Volunteers gathered from many of the tribes until ten thousand were on hand. It was the first time since the conquest of the land under Joshua that the national spirit had been so high.

Word passed quickly to General Sisera that the Israelites were preparing for battle. Without delay trumpets were sounded and the mighty Canaanite army began to assemble. It was an awesome sight to see row after row of nine hundred heavy chariots rumble into formation. Attached to their axles were sharp scythes that whirled a slashing death upon enemy soldiers caught in their path. In short order Sisera's army was assembled sixteen miles away on a plain where the chariots could best operate.

By comparison, Barak's army was no match. He had no cavalry, no chariots, and only ill-armed infantry. Both his officers and their men were inexperienced. However, as mentioned before, God delights to use the weak to defeat the mighty.

Deborah said unto Barak, "Up; for this is the day in which the Lord hath delivered Sisera into thine hand: is not the Lord gone out before thee?" (Judges 4:14).

So the signal was given. From off the mountain the brave Israelites charged. Alerted, Sisera confidently sent word for his chariot army to move out. As the gap closed between the armies, fear must have pulsed in the fast-beating heart of each Hebrew soldier.

The armies were almost within bowshot when a sudden thunderstorm of sleet, hail, and rain burst in over the plain. It flew in the faces of Sisera's soldiers, blinding and confusing them. Horses that pulled chariots became frightened and turned around uncontrollably, sending the whirling scythes into their own men. The plains, which were so suitable to horse-and-chariot combat, now became a sea of mud. Wheels stuck, legs stumbled and slipped, and blood flowed like a river. The Canaanite army turned to flee for their lives. But so heavy was the downpour that the dry bed of the Kishon River became filled with a torrent of rushing water.

Men were washed away and drowned as they attempted to escape. Those who avoided the flood and wild, running horses and chariots were cut down by the pursuing Israelite soldiers. Only General Sisera escaped on foot amidst the confusion. He was later killed by Jael, a woman in whose tent he sought refuge.

Israel had at last thrown off her yoke of Canaanite bondage, and Deborah was hailed as a heroine. But she knew it was God who had given the victory. She wanted all thanksgiving to be presented to Him. With gratefulness in her heart, she wrote a song. Neighbors would sing it; parents would pass it on to future generations. Everyone would become acquainted with the great works of God on behalf of His people through Deborah's song, recorded in Judges 5.

This story is found in Judges 4:1-5:3.

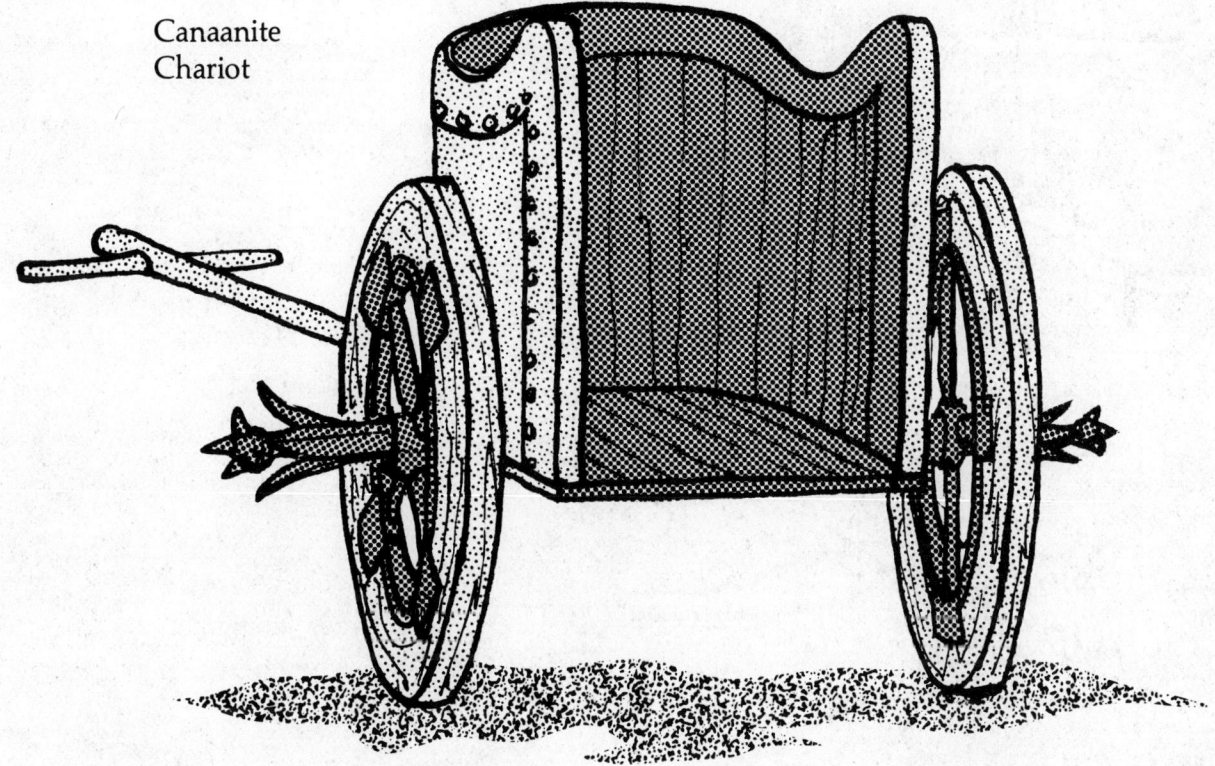

Canaanite Chariot

Thankfulness
of a Hero of the Faith

The air was hot and humid. People were seasick. The 102 Pilgrims crowded on the *Mayflower* had hardly enough room to sit down. For sixty-six days at sea, they had endured these cramped, wretched conditions. Would they ever get to America? Was the England that they had left so bad?

The Church of England in the 1600s had become corrupt. These Pilgrims no longer believed that the church could be purified from within. Only Jesus Christ was the head of His church, not a bishop or a ruler. So they separated themselves and longed to be free to worship as they pleased.

A group of London merchants offered to help the Pilgrims reach America. It seemed to be an anticipated open door, so they entered into an agreement. Families sold their houses and many other possessions. The cash was given to the merchants to help arrange the voyage.

A large, one-hundred-eighty-ton merchantman, the *Mayflower*, was obtained to carry the Pilgrims. The pastor, John Robinson, declared a day of fasting and prayer to help prepare the group spiritually for the arduous journey. At the end of the day, a great farewell dinner was given. Songs were sung, prayers were offered, and God was thanked for His mercies in the past, present, and future.

Travel by sea was at first an adventure to many on board the *Mayflower*. As days lengthened into weeks, the hardships of the trip began to take their toll. Continuous storms caused all the hatches to be closed. This only increased the darkness, the heat, and the musty air below deck. The passengers had to eat dried pork, peas, and fish. Yet, in the grimness of the situation, they continued to pray and thank God for the benefits.

A violent storm hit the ship and caused her to roll viciously from side to side. Little children screamed, wives clung to their husbands, and men feared that the entire ship might capsize. Suddenly a tremendous BOOM resounded throughout the vessel. The huge crossbeam that supported the main mast had cracked and was sagging precariously. In vain, sailors desperately tried to jack the beam back up. Then a Pilgrim remembered the great iron screw of his printing press. Creaking and groaning, the split beam was closed and pressed into place. The ship was saved and ungodly sailors joined the godly Pilgrims in praise and thanksgiving to God.

On November 9, 1620, the welcome cry of "Land Ho!" rang out. Passengers raced to the top deck to see the New World. In spite of the many storms they had encountered, they had been blown fewer than one hundred miles off course, landing near a place the fishermen called Cape Cod. Feeling that God must have wanted them to settle here, they dropped anchor in the natural harbor inside the cape. Upon reaching the sandy shore, prayers of gratefulness were said.

Their first encounter with the native Indians was not peaceful. The Indians tried to scare these intruders away during the first night with their bloodcurdling cries. The next day they attacked the Pilgrims with bow and arrow. Fortunately, no one was killed and the Indians were frightened by musket fire. Again they were grateful to God.

The Pilgrims named the landing site Plymouth after the name of the town that the ship sailed from in England. The soil was rich and fertile. Four spring-fed creeks gave fresh water. On a hill, approximately twenty acres of land had already been cleared and were ready to plant. Yet, mysteriously, no planting had been done for several years. The food they had brought with them would have to sustain them for the long winter to come.

Three long months at sea had weakened the group, and sickness began to set in. Six died in December; eight in January; and in February, they died at a rate of two a day.

Forty-seven people died, nearly one-half of their original number. Thirteen out of eighteen wives died; only three families remained unbroken. Yet, they held their all-loving God blameless for their misery. They knew He understood their problems. God would bless and prosper them in His good time. They were willing to wait because they were confident that God had called them to America.

In the spring God sent the Pilgrims special help in the form of two English-speaking Indians. One helped the settlers learn how to collect beaver pelts, catch eels, stalk deer, plant pumpkins, refine maple syrup, and use herbs for medicine. But most important, he taught them how to plant corn.

The summer of 1621 provided the settlers with a beautiful planting and growing season. The fall's harvest provided more than enough corn to meet the next winter's needs.

So brimming over with gratitude were the Pilgrims that they called for a celebration to be held in October. The local chief who had befriended the peace-loving Pilgrims attended with ninety Indians. They brought five dressed deer and over a dozen fat, wild turkeys. They taught the Pilgrim women how to make hoecakes and a tasty pudding of cornmeal and syrup. They even shared an Indian delicacy called popcorn. The Pilgrims in turn shared vegetables and fruit pies.

The Pilgrims had much to be thankful to God for. He had brought them to America and settled them on specially prepared land. Friendly Indians showed them how to survive in this wild, new world. They were ready for the future. But first, they paused to pray and say thank you to God.

Character Development Challenges

Thankfulness

God commands us to be thankful in everything (1 Thessalonians 5:18). This is difficult to obey, because God sometimes sends us trials and sorrows. A key to the understanding of how to thank God at all times is to realize that God does not tell us to be thankful when we *feel* like it. Rather, our gratefulness is to be based upon an act of our will. We are to give thanks in everything, whether or not we feel like it. Then when we see God work all things together for good, the heartfelt feeling of thanks will come.

Think of five troubles that have occurred in your life recently, such as a friend who has spoken evil of you or a loss of something you highly valued. Sitting down with a pencil and paper, write God a thank-you note. You may not *feel* like it, but do it anyway.

Example

Dear Lord,

I know that You are an all-wise God who never makes a mistake. You are interested in what I do and how I feel. For some reason You have brought this trial my way. (Name the difficulty.)

_____

_____

Thank You, Lord, for this trial. Help me to someday see in this Your goodness to me. In Jesus' name I pray, amen.